D1506081

Creatures of the Forest Habitat

Wild Boars

Harper Avett

PowerKiDS press

New York

Published in 2017 by The Rosen Publishing Group, Inc.
29 East 21st Street, New York, NY 10010

First Edition

Editor: Caitie McAneney
Book Design: Mickey Harmon

Photo Credits: Cover (series logo) iLoveCoffeeDesign/Shutterstock.com; cover, pp. 1, 3, 4, 6, 8, 10, 12, 14, 16, 18, 20, 22—24 (background) BlueRingMedia/Shutterstock.com; cover (boar) David Dirga/Shutterstock.com; pp. 5 (main), 11, 21 (main) Neil Burton/Shutterstock.com; p. 5 (inset) c12/Shutterstock.com; p. 7 (bottom) GGRIGOROV/Shutterstock.com; p. 7 (top) Eduard Kyslynskyy/Shutterstock.com; p. 9 Martchan/Shutterstock.com; p. 13 Budimir Jevtic/Shutterstock.com; p. 15 smishonja/Shutterstock.com; p. 17 Mirek Nowaczyk/Shutterstock.com; p. 19 Marijn Heuts/NiS/Minden Pictures/Getty Images; p. 21 (inset) Irina oxilixo Danilova/Shutterstock.com; p. 22 Eric Isselee/Shutterstock.com.

Cataloging-in-Publication Data

Names: Avett, Harper.
Title: Wild Boars / Harper Avett.
Description: New York : PowerKids Press, 2017. | Series: Creatures of the forest habitat | Includes index.
Identifiers: ISBN 9781499427189 (pbk.) | ISBN 9781499429251 (library bound) | ISBN 9781499427196 (6 pack)
Subjects: LCSH: Wild boar–Juvenile literature.
Classification: LCC QL737.U58 A94 2017 | DDC 599.63'32–dc23

Manufactured in the United States of America

CPSIA Compliance Information: Batch #BW17PK: For Further Information contact Rosen Publishing, New York, New York at 1-800-237-9932

Contents

That's Wild! 4

Boars Around the World. 6

Boars in the Wild. 8

Identifying a Wild Boar 10

Boar Babies. .12

Eating Like a Pig. 14

Sense of Smell. 16

Destructive Animals 18

An Invasive Species 20

At Home in the Forest. 22

Glossary 23

Index 24

Websites 24

That's Wild!

You may have seen pigs on a farm. Long ago, these **domesticated** pigs came from members of the wild boar family. These big **mammals** lived mostly in the forests of Europe and Asia. Today, wild boars are still around. In fact, they've spread to every continent but Antarctica.

Wild boars are very **adaptable** animals. That's what helped them spread around the world. However, in some places, they're considered an **invasive species**. This forest creature can be a real problem. Wild boars are interesting animals. Let's learn more about them!

Forest Friend Facts

Wild boars have one of the widest **ranges** of all land mammals on Earth.

farm pig

wild boar

Do you notice the similarities between the wild boar and the farm pig? What are the differences?

Boars Around the World

For many years, wild boars were found only in Europe and Asia, and some parts of North Africa. Then they were introduced, or brought, to other places.

In the 1500s, Spanish explorer Hernando de Soto brought wild boars to what is now the southeastern United States. The wild boar was a source of food for the European settlers. Many boars roamed free or escaped from their pens, so the species spread to new places. Today, wild boars have been found in at least 45 U.S. states. They were also introduced to Australia and South America.

Forest Friend Facts

Wild boars usually avoid very cold places because it's harder to find roots and leaves in the frozen earth.

Wild boars can live in both warm and cool regions, or places.

7

Boars in the Wild

Wild boars like to live in forests because they provide shelter and food. Roots and leaves are some of the wild boar's favorite foods and the forest is full of them.

Boars aren't picky about where they live. They have other kinds of **habitats**, besides forests. They are known to live in grasslands such as savannas. They also live in wetlands such as marshes. Wild boars live in the Everglades, which is a large area of wetlands in Florida.

Forest Friend Facts

Wild boars are also called "wild hogs."

This wild boar is **foraging** on the forest floor.

Identifying a Wild Boar

Wild boars can grow to more than 7 feet (2.1 m) long. Some reportedly weigh up to 600 pounds (272.2 kg). Most are much smaller than that, though. They have black, brownish, or white hair. The hair is thick and rough. Some boars have patterns in their coat, and some have longer hairs down the center of their back.

Many wild boars have two long teeth that are called tusks. Their tusks can grow as long as 9 inches (22.9 cm).

Forest Friend Facts

Male wild boars are often bigger than females.

Wild boars have long, strong **snouts**.
They use their snouts to dig in the dirt.

11

Boar Babies

Wild boars are known to have many **offspring**. Animals often mate, or come together to make babies, only once a year. Boars in warm regions mate at any time of the year. A mother boar may have four to 12 babies, or piglets, at a time. She may give birth more than two times a year.

Piglets are often lighter in color and have light brown stripes that run down their backs. The mother wild boar lives with her offspring as a family unit.

Forest Friend Facts

When wild boar families join other families, they form huge groups called sounders. Wild boar sounders can have up to 100 members.

Sounders are matriarchal, meaning that one older female boar is the leader of the group. This group is made up of female boars and their offspring. Older male boars are solitary, which means they like to keep to themselves except for when it's time to mate.

Eating Like a Pig

Farm pigs will eat nearly anything, and so will wild boars! That makes them opportunistic eaters. It's one of the reasons they are so adaptable.

Wild boars in warmer climates are most active at night. They forage for roots, nuts, fruit, and other plant parts. They sometimes sneak onto farms and eat the crops. Wild boars eat other animals, including bugs, worms, and small mammals. They sometimes attack livestock, or farm animals. They're also known to eat carrion, or the rotting bodies of dead animals.

Forest Friend Facts

Wild boars have few natural predators. These predators include gray wolves, black bears, cougars, and bobcats. Humans hunt them for food, too.

Wild boars have a big **appetite**!

15

Sense of Smell

Like most animals, wild boars have to search for their food. They don't have a great sense of sight. However, they make up for that with their sense of smell.

The wild boar's sense of smell helps it forage. If you see one in the wild, it will often have its nose to the ground. It can smell things as deep as 25 feet (7.6 m) underground. They can also smell things 5 to 7 miles (8 to 11.3 km) away. That's a strong sense of smell!

Forest Friend Facts

People have long used domesticated pigs to locate and dig up truffles, which are a type of fungus similar to mushrooms. These pigs have the same strong sense of smell wild boars do.

A wild boar's sense of smell can also warn it about nearby danger.

Destructive Animals

A wild boar's sense of smell and large appetite can get it into trouble. They are very destructive, or harmful, to many farms. They can root down into the earth 3 feet (0.9 m) deep. That erodes, or wears away at, soil. They uproot native plants and kill them.

Wild hogs love to eat crops from farms. They can clear fields of crops by turning up the soil and eating along the way. They eat seeds and young plants, and that costs farmers a lot of money.

Forest Friend Facts

Wild boars can carry illnesses and **parasites**. They may pass these on to farm pigs.

When wild boars invade a farm as a group, farmers may lose all their crops. This is especially a problem in Texas.

19

An Invasive Species

Invasive species are animals that aren't native to a region. They have serious effects on the **ecosystem**. That's because native animals have to compete with the new animals for food and water.

Because wild boars cause so much damage in Texas, people are allowed to hunt and kill as many wild boars as they like. Texas law states that if a wild boar is on someone's land, they are the owner of the boar and can do what they want to get rid of it if the boar is causing problems. These people are not required to have a hunting license because wild boars are considered "exotic livestock."

Forest Friend Facts

Although wild boars are invasive, people are not trying to get rid of them entirely. The goal is to control wild boar populations so that they cause fewer problems.

Wild boars are an invasive species in the Florida Everglades. Another invasive species there is the Burmese python.

At Home in the Forest

Many people in the United States aren't big fans of wild boars. They're not native, and they often cause trouble. They are hunted both for food and to control their populations. It's safe to say they are not in danger of dying out anytime soon!

These forest animals are an important native species in other parts of the world. In the United States, however, it's important to keep wild boar populations under control so native species can survive in their natural habitat.

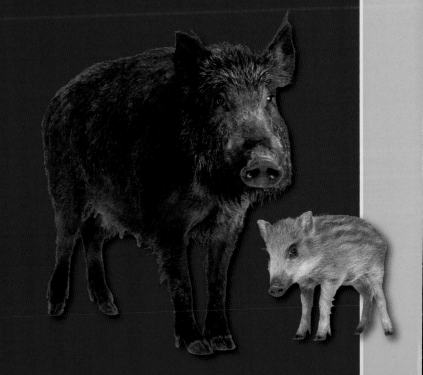

Glossary

adaptable: Able to change in order to live better in certain environments.

appetite: The desire for food.

domesticated: Bred and raised for use by people.

ecosystem: A natural community of living and nonliving things.

forage: To search for food to eat.

habitat: The natural place where an animal or plant lives.

invasive species: Plants or animals from one area that spread quickly in a new area and harm native plants and animals.

mammal: A warm-blooded animal that has a backbone and hair, breathes air, and feeds milk to its young.

offspring: The young of an animal or plant.

parasite: A living thing that lives in, on, or with another living thing and often harms it.

range: The area where something lives.

snout: An animal's nose and mouth.

Index

A

Africa, North, 6
Antarctica, 4
Asia, 4, 6
Australia, 6

C

carrion, 14

E

Europe, 4, 6
Everglades, 8, 21

I

invasive species, 4,
    20, 21

L

leaves, 6, 8
livestock, 14, 20

M

mammal, 4
matriarchal, 13

P

pig, domesticated,
    4, 5, 14,
    16, 18
piglets, 12
predators, 14
python,
    Burmese, 21

R

roots, 6, 8, 14

S

smell, 16, 17, 18
snout, 11
Soto, Hernando
    de, 6
sounders, 12, 13
South America, 6

T

Texas, 19, 20
tusks, 10

U

United States, 6, 22

W

wetlands, 8

Websites

Due to the changing nature of Internet links, PowerKids Press has developed an online list of websites related to the subject of this book. This site is updated regularly. Please use this link to access the list: www.powerkidslinks.com/forest/boar